TELL ME, TREE

All about Trees for Kids

by Gail Gibbons

LITTLE, BROWN AND COMPANY

BOSTON NEW YORK LONDON

To Larry Whiting, who knows all about trees.

Copyright © 2002 by Gail Gibbons

First Edition

Library of Congress Cataloging-in-Publication Data

Gibbons, Gail.
   Tell me, tree: all about trees for kids / by Gail
Gibbons. — 1st ed.
      p. cm.
   ISBN 0-316-30903-6
      1. Trees — Juvenile literature. 2. Trees —
   Identification — Juvenile literature. [1. Trees. 2.
   Trees — Identification.] I. Title.

   QK475.8 .G49 2002
   582.16 — dc21   00-064967

10 9 8 7 6 5 4 3 2 1

TWP

Printed in Singapore

The illustrations for this book were done in watercolors on 140-lb. Arches watercolor paper. The text was set in Janson, and the display type is Pabst.

WHITE
SPRUCE

SUGAR
MAPLE

AMERICAN
BEECH

PIN OAK

TELL ME, TREE . . .
TREES

Trees are woody plants. Their trunks, limbs, and branches are their stems.

BRANCH

LIMB

ELM

TRUNK

TELL ME, TREE . . .

Some trees are small, no more than a few inches tall. Others are big, and still others are huge! Trees grow almost everywhere, except where it is extremely cold or dry or in places at high elevations.

CALIFORNIA REDWOOD

JUNIPER

PAPER BIRCH

SITKA SPRUCE

SUGAR MAPLE

DIFFERENT KINDS OF TREES

SITKA
SPRUCE

CANARY
PALM

MANGROVE

MESQUITE

Trees need light, moisture, soil, and space to grow.
Different trees grow in different environments. Some like
cold weather. Others grow where it is warm year-round.
Some trees like wet places. Others grow in dry climates.

TELL ME, TREE...

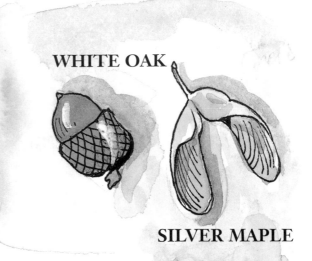

WHITE OAK

SILVER MAPLE

RED OAK

ORANGE SEED

All trees, even the biggest, begin their lives as seeds. These seeds come in different shapes and sizes.

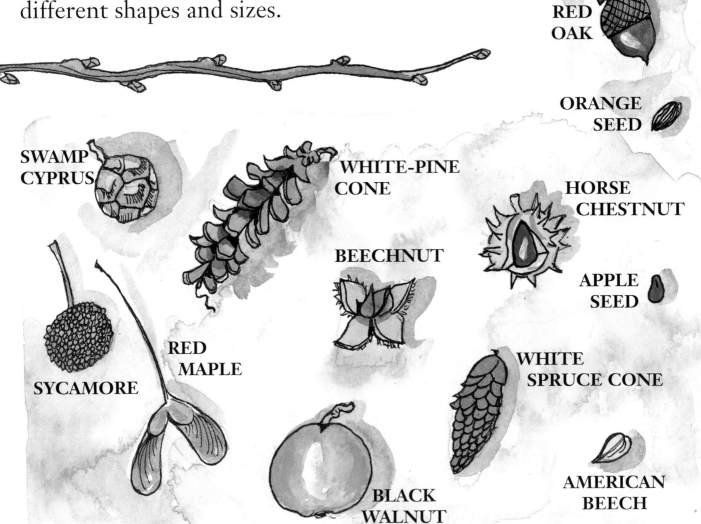

SWAMP CYPRUS

WHITE-PINE CONE

HORSE CHESTNUT

BEECHNUT

APPLE SEED

SYCAMORE

RED MAPLE

WHITE SPRUCE CONE

BLACK WALNUT

AMERICAN BEECH

A baby tree is called a **SEEDLING**.

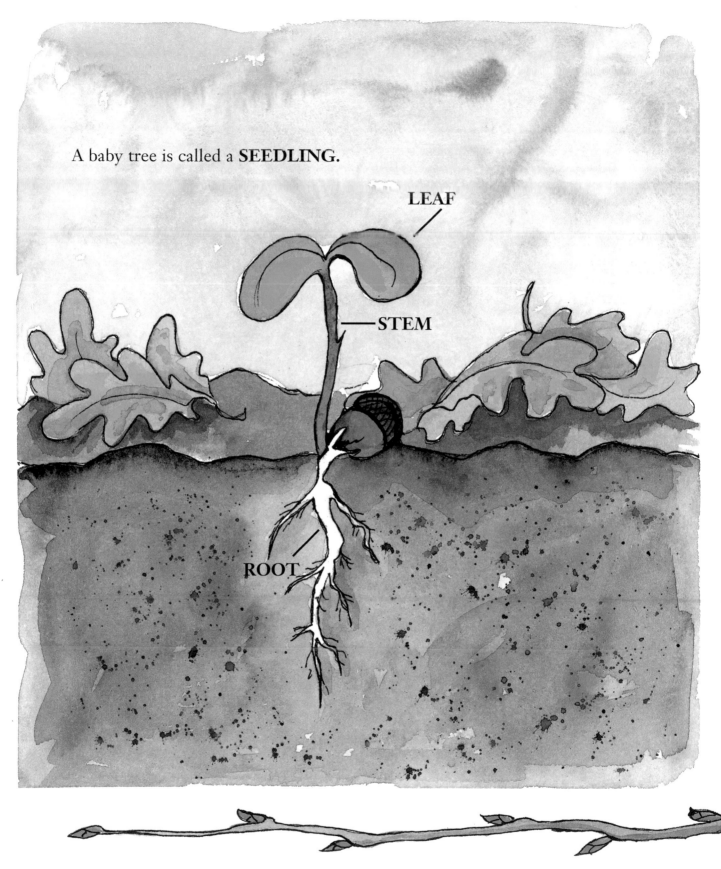

A seed sprouts when a small root begins to grow. As the root absorbs water and minerals, a tiny stem with just two small leaves begins to grow above the soil.

BUD

TRUNK

In time the stem becomes hard enough to be called *wood*.
Small branches begin to appear as buds that turn into tiny
leaves. The hard, woody stem is called a *tree trunk*.

BALSAM POPLAR

A trunk is covered by a hard layer of wood called *bark*. Bark protects trees from weather and insects and animals that attack them. Different kinds of trees have different kinds of bark — hard or soft, thick or thin.

PIN OAK BARK

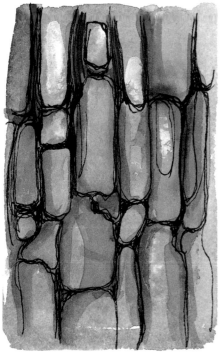

WHITE BIRCH BARK

WHITE PINE BARK

Underneath the bark is a thin layer called the *phloem*. The phloem carries the food made by the leaves to the branches, trunk, and roots of the tree. Next is the *cambium* layer. The cambium layer forms new growth for the trunk of a tree each year.

CAMBIUM

WHITE OAK

PHLOEM

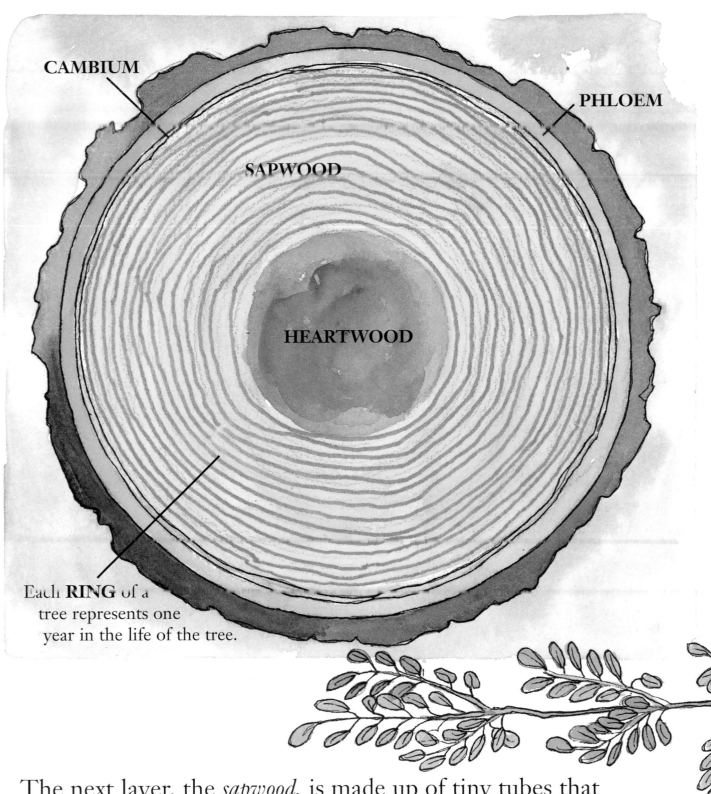

CAMBIUM

PHLOEM

SAPWOOD

HEARTWOOD

Each **RING** of a tree represents one year in the life of the tree.

The next layer, the *sapwood*, is made up of tiny tubes that carry water and minerals, called *sap*, from the roots to the leaves. The center of the tree is called the *heartwood*, dead and solid sapwood that gives a tree its strength to stand.

ROOTS

Roots grow from under the tree trunk down into the ground. Tiny root hairs at the tip of the roots take in water and minerals from the soil to help the tree grow.

ROOT

ROOT
HAIR

ROOTS

Roots anchor a tree in the ground and help hold it upright. Most trees have as many roots below the ground as they have branches above.

LEAVES

The leaves of a tree make food for the tree to grow. The leaves pull up water from the roots and breathe in a gas from the air called *carbon dioxide*. Inside the leaves is a substance called *chlorophyll*.

CHLOROPHYLL

CARBON DIOXIDE
comes from the air.

SILVER MAPLE

The chlorophyll in the leaves gathers energy from the sun. It mixes with water and the carbon dioxide to create food for the tree called *sugar*. This process is *photosynthesis*.

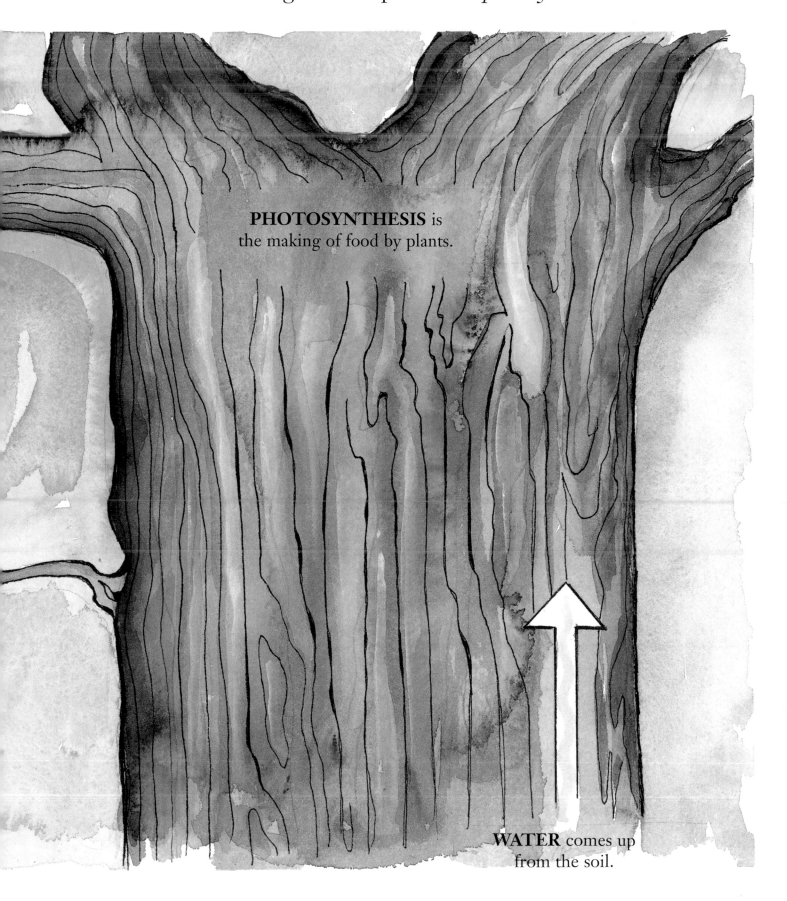

PHOTOSYNTHESIS is
the making of food by plants.

WATER comes up
from the soil.

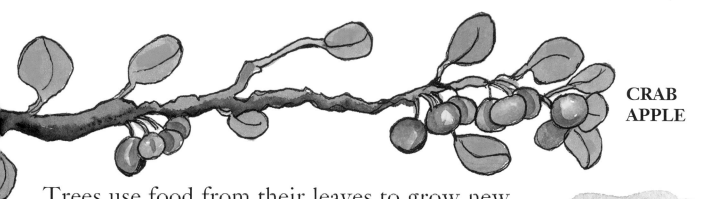

CRAB APPLE

Trees use food from their leaves to grow new wood, branches, twigs, buds, leaves, seeds, nuts, and fruit. The fruit of trees is often sweet from the sugar the leaves make. Trees need their food to stay alive and renew their growth.

ORANGE TREE

CHERRY TREE

APPLE TREE

HORSE CHESTNUT

When leaves make their food they also make a gas called *oxygen*. The leaves release the oxygen into the air. People and animals need oxygen to breathe. Most of the oxygen in the air comes from trees.

TELL ME, TREE . . .

EVERGREENS
are also called
CONIFERS

DOUGLAS FIR

Although leaves come in many different shapes and sizes, there are only two different groups of trees, *evergreen* trees and *broadleaf* trees. Most evergreens have needles that are thin and scalelike. Because most evergreens keep their seeds inside cones, they are also called *conifers*. These trees lose their needles or leaves a few at a time throughout the year.

EASTERN HEMLOCK

EVERGREEN means the tree keeps its needles or leaves all year.

BROADLEAF TREES

COTTONWOOD

The leafy top of a tree is called a **CROWN**.

REDBUD

Broadleaf trees have flatter, wider leaves. Many grow flowers and fruit and produce different kinds of seeds. Most broadleaf trees are *deciduous*. That means they lose their leaves in the autumn. Some leaves turn beautiful colors before they die and fall. In the spring broadleaf trees grow new leaves.

IDENTIFYING TREES

SASSAFRAS

TULIP TREE

WEEPING WILLOW

YELLOW BIRCH

You can identify a tree by looking at the shapes of its leaves. Some leaves are smooth-edged, some are rough-edged. Some are very big and broad. Others are small and thin.

BLACK LOCUST TREE

LIVE OAK

WEEPING WILLOW

TAMARACK

COTTONWOOD

LOMBARDY POPLAR

WHITE BIRCH

ELM

SWEET CHERRY

RED OAK

BEECH

SUGAR MAPLE

WHITE PINE

PIN OAK

CANARY PALM

BLACK WALNUT

TELL ME MORE, TREE . . .

Trees are used in many ways. They are harvested for their wood, to build homes and to make furniture, crates, paper, pencils . . . thousands of things we use every day. We eat the nuts and fruit grown on trees, too. Many animals and birds make their homes in trees.

NUTS

Millions of trees are cut down each year. It is important to harvest trees carefully and to plant new ones. Future growth is important because trees make oxygen for people and animals to breathe. Their roots hold soil together to keep it from eroding. Also, they make the world a beautiful place to live.

MAKE YOUR OWN TREE
Collect your favorite leaves and identify them.

PRESSING A LEAF

Place the leaf between two pieces of newspaper.

Pile one or two heavy books on top.

After one week the leaf should be flat and dry. You can glue it down in your Tree Identification Book. Next to the leaf, write the name of the tree it came from.

WHITE OAK

LEAF RUBBING

Place the leaf between two pieces of unlined paper on a smooth, hard surface. Gently rub a pencil or crayon back and forth on the upper sheet until the leaf appears.

Cut the rubbing out and glue it in your book. Next to the rubbing, write the name of the tree the leaf came from.

AMERICAN BEECH

IDENTIFICATION BOOK

BARK RUBBING

Tape or tie a piece of strong, thin paper to the trunk of the tree. Slowly rub the thick side of a crayon over the paper in one direction.

Cut the rubbing out and glue it in your book. Label the name of the tree next to it.

AMERICAN ELM BARK

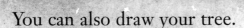
You can also draw your tree.

SUGAR MAPLE LEAF

Sept. 10th

BARK RUBBING Sept. 8

SUGAR MAPLE SEED

Drawing of Sugar Maple Tree

SUGAR MAPLE TWIG

If your tree has flat seeds you can glue them in the book, too. Or you can try drawing them.

Each page can identify a different tree. You can even date when you identified the leaves.

TELL ME LOTS MORE ABOUT TREES . . .

 • The Ginkgo biloba is an ancient tree that has been around for 350 million years.

 • Trees are the largest living things in the world.

 • Trees cover about a third of the Earth's land surface.

• The heaviest trees are giant sequoias. They are believed to weigh 2 million tons and are up to 270 feet tall.

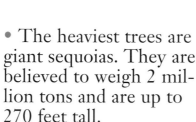 • In the fall some leaves turn colors because chlorophyll stops being produced. As the green disappears, the leaves turn the colors of the other chemicals the leaves make. Look around! Red leaves, gold leaves, orange leaves . . .

 • The oldest tree on record is a bristlecone pine on Mt. Wheeler, Nevada. It was 4,900 years old when it was cut down.

 • Trying to use less paper is a good way to save trees.

 • The tallest trees in the world are California redwoods. They can grow to be 400 feet tall!

 • If you can, have fun planting your own tree!

 • Most leaves are thin. The dark lines are the veins of a leaf. They carry food and water.

 • In the spring, when the days get warm but the nights are still cold, some people make maple syrup from sugar maple trees. They boil the sap they gather from the trees until it becomes sweet maple syrup.

 • Recycle the paper you use.

 • In the winter many trees take a rest. Although they formed new buds in the fall, they lie dormant until spring. In the spring the trees' buds will make new leaves.